...Hazel has offered us the love of J... orable presentation, with the same ... the joy of children, and—dare I s... who look on the world with fresh ... with an accuracy of scansion and fi... ing book...and will give...pleasure...over and over again.

Anne Atkins
Broadcaster, "Agony Aunt" to the Daily Mail,
TV Presenter, actress, and author

This is a glorious book! Most unusual and refreshing. I'll enjoy it for years to come as I share it with my grandkids.

Jennifer Rees-Larcombe
Author

This book is a delightful family nursery rhyme book, familiar to most of us who grew up reciting them. These alternative verses provide parents and children's church leaders with a lovely way to introduce the Gospel to little ones and sometimes to parents alike. I wish it had been available when my children were small!

Fiona Castle OBE (widow of Roy Castle)
Author, chairman of Activate

Nursery Rhymes seem to stay in our minds forever. Now, with this beautifully crafted, inspirational book of rhymes, we can also leave vital Bible and God truths, with our children, grandchildren, friends and pupils, in a day and age when so many little ones don't get to hear the important message and teachings of a God who loves them!

Row Robinson
Youth and Children's worker in schools,
Koinonia Praise Parties and Koinonia Kamps

A fantastic way of teaching the Bible and its principles to children in a simple and easy to learn style! Also dedicated to a wonderful woman who strived to teach the Bible to children and families.

Hannah Nelson
Senior Youth Worker at St. Michael's
Church, Aberystwyth, Wales

Heaven's
Humpties

Heaven's Humpties

Nursery Rhymes for God's Family

By Hazel Butler

TATE PUBLISHING & *Enterprises*

Published by Tate Publishing & Enterprises, LLC
127 E. Trade Center Terrace | Mustang, Oklahoma 73064 USA
1.888.361.9473 | www.tatepublishing.com

Tate Publishing is committed to excellence in the publishing industry. The company reflects the philosophy established by the founders, based on Psalm 68:11,
"The Lord gave the word and great was the company of those who published it."

Book design copyright © 2007 by Tate Publishing, LLC. All rights reserved.
Cover design & Illustrations by Kathy Hoyt
Interior design by Leah LeFlore

Published in the United States of America

ISBN: 978-1-60462-143-3
1. Youth & Children: Non-fiction Christian
2. Juvenile Non-fiction: Poetry: Nursery Rhymes

07.11.06

Dedication

These nursery rhymes are written in loving memory of Hilary Skinner, who died on 16 February 2005.

Hilary dedicated her life to bringing God's love to children—her own children and grandchildren, the children she fostered, and the hundreds of children with whom she shared her faith so enthusiastically.

I trust she would have enjoyed these poems and used them in imaginative and effective ways to teach about the love of her Lord and Saviour to the hoards of children who always seemed to surround her.

Introduction

Heaven's Humpties follow as nearly as possible the same metre, rhythm, and rhyming as the traditional nursery rhymes. They are firmly based on scriptural teaching, and the texts from which the teaching is drawn are identified next to the relevant rhyme. The Bible references indicate the whole passage of Scripture that relates to the rhyme, but only the most relevant verses are written out in full.

The simple rhymes in *Part 1* are suitable for younger children to read alone or alongside an adult. The more sophisticated rhymes in the second half will be appreciated more by older children and adults. All are suitable for use as a resource for school assemblies, holiday clubs, all-age worship, etc.

Foreword

There is a long and honourable tradition in the use of lampoon and satire as a means of expressing truth. I tripped and fell into this tradition more than twenty years ago after a stress illness benevolently stripped away my capacity for editing out things that other people might find inappropriate or shocking. I was, to say the least, intrigued to discover that exaggeration and strategic distortion could produce such clear and clean windows to reality. Given Jesus' unequivocal statement that the truth will set us free, I am a little surprised at my own surprise, but there we are.

It can take years for people like me—like us—to actually open our eyes. In this context, I have "had a go" at nursery rhymes myself in the past, but only a very small number compared with Hazel's collection in this book. As you read them, you will quickly understand that the writer is a follower of Jesus who is passionately committed to communicating a faith that means the world and more to her. There is, of course, no compulsion, divine or otherwise, for those of us who call ourselves writers or artists to produce specifically Christian material, but when we do write directly about our faith, we should always be on the lookout for fresh means of expression.

Hazel has certainly succeeded in this respect, and I do hope that you will enjoy and appreciate all of *Heaven's Humpties*.

Adrian Plass
International Speaker and Author of
Bacon Sandwiches and Salvation

Table of Contents

Part 1
For younger members of God's family

Part 2
For Older Members of God's Family

Part 1

For Younger Members of God's Family

Twinkle, Twinkle

Twinkle, twinkle little star;
how I wonder what you are!
Up above the world so high,
like a diamond in the sky.
Twinkle, twinkle little star;
how I wonder what you are!

Twinkle, Twinkle

Twinkle, twinkle great big star;
how I wonder what you are!
Up above the world so high,
Sends a message from the sky.
Twinkle, twinkle great big star;
Christ is born! So shout, "Hurrah!"

"...the star...went ahead of them and stopped over the place where the child was."

Matthew 2:9–10

"I bring you good news that will bring great joy to all people. The Saviour, yes the Messiah, the Lord, has been born today..."

Luke 2:10

Hark, Hark, the Dogs Do Bark

Hark, hark, the dogs do bark,
the beggars are coming to town;
some in rags, and some in jags,
and one in a velvet gown.

Hark, Hark, How Angels Mark

Hark, hark how angels mark
that Jesus is coming to earth!
Those in rags, or driving jags,
all hear of His wondrous birth.

Hark, hark, within your heart,
He tenderly bids you to come!
"Rich and poor, with less or more,
Just come, my dear child, come home!"

"Suddenly, an angel of the Lord appeared among them, and the radiance of the Lord's glory surrounded them...he said. 'I bring you good news that will bring great joy to all people. The Saviour—yes, the Messiah, the Lord—has been born today in Bethlehem.'"

Luke 2:9–11

"Suddenly, the angel was joined by a vast host of others—the armies of heaven—praising God and saying, 'Glory to God in highest heaven, and peace on earth to those with whom God is pleased.'"

Luke 2:13–14

"There is no longer Jew or Gentile, slave or free, male and female. For you are all one in Christ Jesus. And now that you belong to Christ, you are the true children of Abraham."

Galatians 3:28–29

"Jesus said, 'Come to me, all of you who are weary and carry heavy burdens, and I will give you rest.'"

Matthew 11:28

Little Boy Blue

Little boy blue, come blow your horn!
The sheep's in the meadow,
the cow's in the corn.
Where is the boy who looks after the sheep?
He's under the haycock fast asleep.
Will you waken him? No, not I!
For if I do, he's sure to cry!

Little Boy Blue

Listen! It's true! Come blow your horn!
The sheep need a shepherd,
and now He's been born.
Where is the One who'll look after His sheep?
He lies in a manger fast asleep.
Will you worship Him? Tell me why!
'Cos He's your king, the Lord most high!

"And when he saw the crowds, he had compassion on them, for they were confused and helpless, like sheep without a shepherd."

Matthew 9:36

"So my people are wandering like lost sheep; they are attacked because they have no shepherd."

Zechariah 10:2

"[Jesus said], 'I am the good shepherd.'"

John 10:11

"…an angel of the Lord appeared…He said…'The Saviour, yes the Messiah, the Lord—has been born today in Bethlehem…. You will find a baby wrapped snugly in strips of cloth, lying in a manger.'"

Luke 2:8–15

"The shepherds went back glorifying and praising God for all they had heard and seen. It was just as the angel had told them."

Luke 2:20

Christmas Is Coming

Christmas is coming,
the geese are getting fat.
Please put a penny
in the old man's hat.
If you haven't got a penny
a ha'penny will do;
if you haven't got a ha'penny
then God bless you!

Christmas Is Coming

Christmas is coming,
The gifts are getting wrapped.
We see so many
in old Santa's sack!
Jesus hadn't got a penny,
He lost all for you
so that you could be forgiven
and God bless you!

"Though He was God … He gave up His divine privileges … took the humble position of a slave."

Philippians 2:6–8

"Foxes have dens to live in, and birds have nests, but the son of Man has no place even to lay his head."

Matthew 8:20

"God's free gift leads to our being made right with God."

Romans 5:16

Little Bo-Peep

Little Bo-Peep
has lost her sheep
and doesn't know
where to find them.
Leave them alone
and they'll come home
dragging their tails behind them.

Jesus Did Weep

Jesus did weep;
He lost his sheep;
and came down from
Heav'n to find them.
They're not alone,
since they've come home,
leaving their failures behind them.

"If a man has a hundred sheep and one of them wanders away, what will he do? ... Won't he go out to search for the one that is lost? ... It is not my heavenly father's will that even one of these little ones should perish."

Matthew 18:12–14

"And be sure of this: I am with you always, even to the end of the age."

Matthew 28:20

" ... consider yourselves to be dead to the power of sin and alive to God through Christ Jesus."

Romans 6:11

Little Jack Horner

Little Jack Horner
sat in the corner
eating his Christmas pie.
He put in his thumb
and pulled out a plum,
and said, "What a good boy am I!"

Little Jack Horner

Little Jack Horner
sat in the corner
eating his Christmas pie.
He thought of the room
he'd swept with a broom,
and said, "What a good boy am I!"

Little Jack Horner
sat in the corner
eating his Christmas pie.
He thought of his spite,
his temper and bite,
and said, "What a bad boy am I!"

Little Jack Horner
sat in the corner,
eating his Christmas pie.
He thought of God's Son
and how He had come,
and said, "What a loved boy am I!"

"I want to do what is right, but I can't. I want to do what is good, but I don't. I don't want to do what is wrong, but I do it anyway…Who will free me?…Thank God! The answer is in Jesus Christ our Lord."

Romans 7:18–25

"For God loved the world so much that He gave his one and only Son, so that everyone who believes in Him will not perish but have eternal life."

John 3:16

Mary Had a Little Lamb

Mary had a little lamb,
its fleece was white as snow;
and everywhere that Mary went
the lamb was sure to go.
It followed her to school one day;
that was against the rule.
It made the children laugh and play
to see a lamb at school.

Jesus Had a Little Lamb

Jesus had a little lamb,
His heart was black as soot;
and everywhere this bad lamb went
a wrong foot he would put.
He followed his own willful way
and didn't keep God's rule,
and other lambs he'd lead astray
whilst acting like a fool.

Jesus loved this little lamb,
and washed him white as snow;
now every time that Jesus calls
the lamb is sure to go.
He follows Him real close each day
because he made a choice;
no longer going his own way,
He'd follow Jesus' voice.

"He calls his own sheep by name and leads them out. After he has gathered his own flock, he walks ahead of them, and they follow him because they know his voice."

John 10:3–4

"All of us, like sheep, have strayed away. We have left God's paths to follow our own."

Isaiah 53:6

"Fools think their own way is right."

Proverbs 12:5

" … associate with fools and get in trouble."

Proverbs 13:20

"He washed away our sins, giving us a new birth and new life through the Holy Spirit."

Titus 3:5

There Was a Crooked Man

There was a crooked man
who walked a crooked mile;
he found a crooked sixpence
upon a crooked style.
He had a crooked cat
who found a crooked mouse.
They all lived together
in a little crooked house.

There Was a Crooked Man

There was a crooked man
who had a crooked wife;
their crooked thoughts and actions
led to a crooked life.
They had some crooked kids,
whose crooked ways unfurled;
they all lived together
in a sad and crooked world.

The Straight Man up in Heaven
sent John to pave the way,
to straighten out the highway,
prepare for Straight Man's day.
So all the crooked kids,
the crooked man and wife
could all live together
in a new and straightened life.

"The guilty walk a crooked path; the innocent travel a straight road."

Proverbs 21:8

"...they began to think up foolish ideas...as a result, their minds became dark and confused...they did vile and degrading things...their lives became full of every kind of wickedness...worse yet, they encourage others to do them, too."

Romans 1:21–32

"The prophet was speaking about John when he said, 'He is a voice shouting in the wilderness, 'Prepare the way for the Lord's coming! Clear the road for Him!''"

Matthew 3:1–17

"For the sin of this one man, Adam, brought death to many. But even greater is God's wonderful grace and His gift of forgiveness to many through this other man, Jesus Christ."

Romans 5:15–19

Baa Baa Black Sheep

Baa Baa black sheep,
have you any wool?
Yes sir, yes sir,
three bags full!
One for the master
and one for the dame,
and one for the little boy
who lives down the lane!

Baa Baa Black Sheep

Baa baa black sheep,
have you gone astray?
Yes sir, yes sir,
lost my way!
Here comes the Shepherd
Who calls you by name,
and home, on his shoulders safe,
He brings you again!

"Do not be afraid … I have called you by name; you are mine."

Isaiah 43:1

"If a man has a hundred sheep and one of them gets lost, what will he do? Won't he leave the ninety-nine others in the wilderness and go to search for the one that is lost until he finds it? And when he has found it, he will joyfully carry it home on his shoulders."

Luke 15:4–7

Simple Simon

Simple Simon met a pie man
going to the fair.
Said Simple Simon to the pie man,
"Let me taste your ware."
Said the pie man unto Simon,
"Show me first your penny!"
Said Simple Simon to the pie man,
"Sir, I have not any!"

Troubled Tristan

Troubled Tristan met a Christian
on his way to Heav'n.
Said Troubled Tristan to the Christian,
"Let me be forgiv'n!"
Said the Christian unto Tristan,
"Does not cost a penny!"
Said Troubled Tristan to the Christian,
"But my sins are many!"

Said the Christian unto Tristan,
"Do you trust good deeds?"
Said Troubled Tristan to the Christian,
"All I have is needs!"
Said the Christian unto Tristan,
"Christ forgives your sin then!"
Said Troubled Tristan to the Christian,
"Sir, I can begin, then!"

"All of this is a gift from God, who brought us back to Himself through Christ."

2 Corinthians 5:18

"My grace is all you need. My power works best in weakness."

2 Corinthians 12:9

"And since it is through God's kindness, then it is not by their good works. For in that case, God's grace would not be what it really is—free and undeserved."

Romans 11:6

Ring a Ring o' Roses

Ring a ring o' roses;
a pocket full of posies;
a'tishoo! A'tishoo!
We all fall down!

Ring a Ring o' Roses

Ring a ring o' roses;
our doubts, our fears, our poses;
"What if you? What if you?"
We all fall down!

Ring a ring o' roses;
God's promise is He knows us.
He lifts you! He lifts you!
We all get up!

" …he who doubts is like a wave of the sea, blown and tossed by the wind."

James 1:6 (RSV)

" …You can go to bed without fear…for the Lord is your security."

Proverbs 3:24–26

"I know my own sheep, and they know me."

John 10:14–15

" …Even youths will become weak and tired, and young men will fall…But those who trust in the Lord will find new strength. They will soar high …They will walk and not faint."

Isaiah 40:29–31

Rub a Dub Dub

Rub a dub dub,
three men in a tub;
and how do you think they got there?
The butcher, the baker,
the candlestick maker,
they all jumped out of a rotten potato.
'Twas enough to make a man stare.

Rub a Dub Dub

Rub a dub dub,
all sorts in God's club;
and how do you think they got there?
Be it butcher or baker,
from here to Jamaica,
they all jumped into the arms of their Maker,
and trusted themselves to His care.

"There is no longer Jew or Gentile, slave or free, male and female. For you are all one in Christ Jesus. And now that you belong to Christ, you are the true children of Abraham."

Galatians 3:28–29

"Jesus said, 'Come to me, all of you who are weary and carry heavy burdens, and I will give you rest.'"

Matthew 11:28

Hot Cross Buns

Hot cross buns!
Hot cross buns!
One a penny,
two a penny,
hot cross buns!

Tell it to your master,
tell it to your sons.
One a penny,
two a penny,
hot cross buns!

Hot Cross Buns

Hot cross buns!
Hot cross buns!
Tell of Heaven,
sins forgiven!
Hot cross buns!

Tell it to your daughters,
tell it to your sons.
Tell of Heaven,
sins forgiven!
Hot cross buns!

"He made peace with everything in heaven and on earth by means of Christ's blood on the cross."

Colossians 1:20

"The good news has been preached all over the world, and I ... have been appointed ... to proclaim it."

Colossians 1:23

Mary, Mary, Quite Contrary

Mary, Mary, quite contrary,
how does your garden grow?
With silver bells and cockle shells
and pretty maids all in a row.

Mary, Mary, Quite Contrary

Mary, Mary, quite contrary,
how does your garden grow?
When some seeds fall
on path and wall,
the little birds peck as they grow.

Mary, Mary, quite contrary,
how does your garden grow?
With shallow soil,
despite your toil,
the sun burns the seeds as they grow.

Mary, Mary, quite contrary,
how does your garden grow?
For your loose seeds
fall in the weeds,
which choke them so they cannot grow.

Mary, Mary, not contrary,
how does your garden grow?
Your seeds take birth
in rich, moist earth,
and pretty flowers flourish and grow.

"A farmer went out to plant some seeds…some seed fell on a footpath, and the birds came and ate them. Other seeds fell on shallow soil…the plants soon wilted under the hot sun.… Other seeds fell among thorns that choked out the tender plants. Still other seeds fell on fertile soil, and they produced a crop that was…a hundred times as much as had been planted!"

"The seed that fell on the footpath represents those who hear the message…and don't understand it. The evil one…snatches away the seed…The seed on the rocky soil represents those who hear the message and immediately receive it with joy. But since they don't have deep roots…they fall away as soon as they have problems…The seed that fell among the thorns represents those who hear God's word, but…the message is crowded out by…worries…and the lure of wealth…The seed that fell on good soil represents those who truly hear and understand God's word and produce a harvest…"

Matthew 13:3–8, 19–23

Polly, Put the Kettle On

Polly, put the kettle on!
Polly, put the kettle on!
Polly, put the kettle on!
    We'll all have tea.

Sukie, take it off again!
Sukie, take it off again!
Sukie, take it off again!
They've all gone home!

Polly, Get the Bible Out

Polly, get the Bible out!
Polly, get the Bible out!
Polly, get the Bible out!
    God speaks to me.

Satan takes it back again,
Satan takes it back again,
Satan takes it back again,
"Don't trust that tome!"

Polly, get the Bible out!
Polly, get the Bible out!
Polly, get the Bible out!
    It sets me free!

"Until I get there, focus on reading the Scriptures to the church, encouraging the believers, and teaching them."

1 Timothy 4:13

"(The serpent) asked the woman, 'Did God really say you must not eat the fruit...?...You won't die!'"

Genesis 3:1

"All scripture is inspired by God and is useful to teach us what is true and to make us realize what is wrong in our lives. It corrects us when we are wrong and teaches us to do what is right. God uses it to prepare and equip His people to do every good work."

2 Timothy 3:16–17

"And you will know the truth, and the truth will set you free."

John 8:32

There Was an Old Woman

There was an old woman
who lived in a shoe.
She had so many children,
she didn't know what to do.
She gave them some broth without any bread;
she whipped them all soundly
and put them to bed.

There Was a Rich Ruler

There was a rich ruler,
too good to be true.
He kept so many rulings
but didn't know what to do.
He wanted God's life to which Jesus said,
"Be stripped of your wealth, and
come, follow instead!"

"Someone came to Jesus with this question: 'Teacher, what good deed must I do to have eternal life?'...Jesus replied...'If you want to receive eternal life, keep the commandments.'...'I've obeyed all these commandments,' the young man replied, 'What else must I do?' Jesus told him, 'If you want to be perfect, go and sell all your possessions and give the money to the poor, and you will have treasure in Heaven. Then, come, follow me.' But when the young man heard this, he went away very sad, for he had many possessions."

Matthew 19:16–22

It's Raining, It's Pouring

It's raining, it's pouring,
the old man is snoring.
He bumped his head
on the end of the bed
and couldn't get up in the morning!

It's Raining, It's Pouring

It's raining, it's pouring,
the old man is snoring.
Get up and pray,
though you're tempted to stay,
and it's hard to get up in the morning.

"Keep watch and pray, so that you will not give into temptation. For the spirit is willing, but the body is weak!"

Matthew 26:41

Jack Be Nimble

Jack be nimble, Jack be quick!
Jack jump over the candlestick!

Jack Be Nimble

Jack, his little light he hid,
jacketed by a basket lid!

Jack, be nimble, Jack be quick!
Jack it up on a candlestick!

Jack be gentle, Jack be good!
Jack! Shine out as your candle would!

Jack! Let people see your ways,
Jack sin in, and then give God praise!

"No one lights a lamp and then puts it under a basket. Instead, a lamp is placed on a stand, where it gives light to everyone in the house. In the same way, let your good deeds shine out for all to see, so that everyone will praise your heavenly Father."

Matthew 5:15–16

Little Miss Muffet

Little Miss Muffet
sat on a tuffet
eating her curds and whey.
Along came a spider
who sat down beside her
and frightened Miss Muffet away.

Little Miss Muffet

Little Miss Muffet
sat on a tuffet;
reading God's Word, she'd pray.
Along came the devil
who whispered his evil,
and tried hard to lead her astray!

Little Miss Muffet
sat on a tuffet;
reading God's Word, she'd pray.
She'd quote from the Word, and
she knew she'd been heard, for
it frightened the devil away!

"Stay alert! Watch out for your great enemy, the devil. He prowls around like a roaring lion, looking for someone to devour."

1 Peter 5:8

" ...Take the sword of the Spirit, which is the word of God."

Ephesians 6:17

"Jesus was ...tempted ...by the Devil ...and Jesus told him, '...The Scriptures say.'...then the devil went away."

Matthew 4:1–11

This Little Piggy

This little piggy went to market;
this little piggy stayed at home;
this little piggy had roast beef,
and this little piggy had none;
and this little piggy went
"Wee wee wee," all the way home.

This Little Christian

This little Christian went to market;
this little Christian stayed at home;
this little Christian had roast beef,
but this little Christian had none!
So rich little Christian said,
"Please, please, please, eat at my home!"

"And all the believers met together in one place and shared every thing that they had...with those in need...and shared their meals with great joy and generosity."

Acts 2:44–46

Humpty Dumpty

Humpty Dumpty
sat on the wall;
Humpty Dumpty
had a great fall.
All the king's horses
and all the king's men
couldn't put Humpty
together again.

Haughty Naughty

Haughty, naughty,
that's like us all;
Haughty, naughty,
see our great fall!
All our good causes
and all our wise men
couldn't put us back
together again.

Sought me, caught me,
Christ gave His all;
Sought me, caught me,
broke my great fall.
Bound evil forces
by dying and then,
rising He put me
together again.

"Pride goes before destruction, and haughtiness before a fall."

Proverbs 16:18

"No one can ever be made right by doing what the law commands ... For everyone has sinned; we all fall short of God's glorious standard ... People are made right with God when they believe that Jesus sacrificed His life."

Romans 3:19–28

"In this way He disarmed the spiritual rulers and authorities. He shamed them publicly by His victory over them on the cross."

Colossians 2:15

" ... Abraham believed in the God who brings the dead back to life and who creates new things out of nothing."

Romans 4:17

Round and Round the Garden

Round and round the garden
like a teddy bear.
One step, two steps
tickly under there!

Round and Round the Garden

Round and round the garden,
wandering in prayer.
One step, two steps,
thoughts flit everywhere!

Christ, whilst in the garden,
prayed the perfect prayer.
"Fulfill your will;
in your work I share."

"...We don't know what God wants us to pray for...but the Spirit pleads for us believers in harmony with God's own will."

Romans 8:26–27

"Jesus went to the olive grove...praying, 'My Father! If it is possible let this cup of suffering be taken from me. Yet I want your will to be done, not mine...If this cup cannot be taken away unless I drink it, your will be done.'"

Matthew 26:36–43

The Grand Old Duke of York

The grand old duke of York
he had ten thousand men.
He marched them up
to the top of the hill
and he marched them down again.
And when they were up they were up;
and when they were down they were down;
and when they were only half way up
they were neither up nor down!

Our Mighty God in Heaven

Our mighty God in Heaven
He has ten thousand men
who'll sing His praise
to the end of their days
and will sing in Heav'n again.
For he who is down can go up;
'cos He who was up has come down;
and he who is feeling halfway up
will be raised right up from down!

"Praise the Lord, you angels ... Yes, praise the Lord, you army of angels who serve Him and do His will! Praise the Lord, everything He has created, everything in all His kingdom. Let all that I am praise the Lord!"

Psalm 103:20–22

" ... The Scriptures say, 'When he ascended to the heights, he led a crowd of captives and gave gifts to his people.' Notice that it says 'he ascended.' This clearly means that Christ also descended to our lowly world, and the same one who descended is the one who ascended higher than all the heavens, so that he might fill the entire universe with himself."

Ephesians 4:8–10

" ... Even though we were dead ... He gave us life when He raised Christ from the dead ... He raised us from the dead along with Christ and seated us with Him in heavenly realms ..."

Ephesians 2:4–6

"The LORD upholds all those who fall and lifts up all who are bowed down."

Psalm 145v14 (NIV)

Two Little Dicky Birds

Two little dicky birds
sitting on the wall;
one named Peter,
the other named Paul.
Fly away, Peter!
Fly away, Paul!
Come back, Peter!
Come back, Paul!

Two Willing Missionaries

Two willing missionaries
sitting in the pew;
one named Peter,
the other named Pru.
Fly away, Peter!
Fly away, Pru!
Till you're back we'll
pray for you.

" ...Pray that I will proclaim this message as clearly as I should."

Colossians 4:4

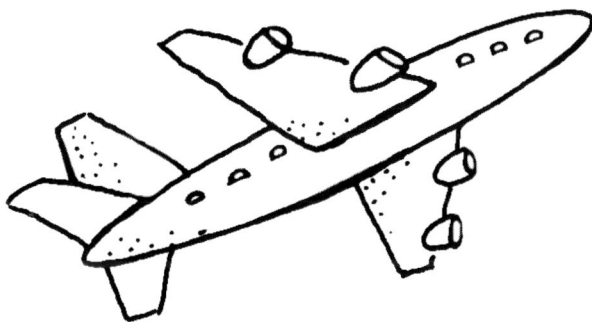

Little Tommy Tucker

Little Tommy Tucker
sings for his supper.
What will you give him?
Brown bread and butter.

Little Tommy Tucker

Little Tommy Tucker
sings for his supper.
What will you give him?
Brown bread and butter.

Never would you offer
stones for his supper,
rather than give him
cakes and a cuppa!

How much more will God then
care for His children,
longing to give them
good gifts from Heaven?

"You parents—if your children ask for a loaf of bread, do you give them a stone instead? Or if they ask for a fish, do you give them a snake? Of course not! So if you sinful people know how to give good gifts to your children, how much more will your heavenly Father give good gifts to those who ask Him?"

Matthew 7:9

Sing a Song of Sixpence

Sing a song of sixpence,
a pocket full of rye.
Four and twenty blackbirds
baked in a pie.
When the pie was opened
the birds began to sing.
Now wasn't that a dainty dish
to set before the king?

Sing a Song to Jesus

Sing a song to Jesus;
we worship Him on high;
voices lifted upwards
as spirits fly!
Now our hearts are opened,
His praises we can sing.
Now, isn't that a dainty dish
to set before our king?

"The sounds of joy and laughter.... The joyful voices ...will be heard again, along with the joyful songs of people bringing thanksgiving offerings to the Lord."

Jeremiah 33:11

"Young men and young women, old men and children. Let them all praise the name of the Lord. For His name is very great ... He has made his people strong."

Psalm 148:12–14

Hark! Hark! The Dogs Do Bark

Hark, hark, the dogs do bark;
the beggars are coming to town;
some in rags, and some in jags
and one in a velvet gown.

Hark! Hark! Just Hear the Lark

Hark, hark! Just hear the lark!
God cares for the birds of the air.
You're preferred to flocks of birds.
God numbers your every hair!

Hark, hark, you heard the lark!
Now think of the lilies and grass.
None can sow, or plough or hoe;
their beauty you can't surpass.

Hark, hark, just like the lark,
God cares for these blooms as they grow;
clothes and feeds and meets their needs,
though into the fire they go.

"Look at the birds! They don't plant or harvest or store food in barns, for your heavenly father feeds them. And aren't you far more valuable to Him than they are? ... And why worry about clothing? Look at the lilies of the field and how they grow ... Solomon in all his glory was not dressed as beautifully as they are ... and if God cares so wonderfully for wild flowers that are here today and thrown into the fire tomorrow, He will certainly care for you."

Matthew 6:26–33

"What is the price of five sparrows? ... God does not forget a single one of them. And the very hairs on your head are all numbered ... You are more valuable to God than a whole flock of sparrows."

Luke 12:6–7

Part 2

For Older Members of God's Family

Rock-a-Bye Baby

Rock-a-bye baby
on the treetop,
when the wind blows the cradle will rock;
when the bough breaks the cradle will fall,
down will come baby, cradle, and all.

Rock the Christ Baby

Rock the Christ Baby,
Here our fears stop.
When His wind blows, earth truly will rock;
When His power makes all evil to fall,
down will come Satan, death, sin, and all.

"Then Jesus shouted out again, and He released His spirit. At that moment...the earth shook, rocks split apart, and tombs opened. The bodies of many godly men and women who had died were raised from the dead.... The Roman officer said, 'This man truly was the Son of God!'"

Matthew 27:50–52

"Suddenly, there was a sound from heaven like the roaring of a mighty windstorm...When they heard the loud noise, everyone...[was] bewildered...Then Peter...shouted..."In the last days,' God says, 'I will pour out my Spirit upon all people...I will cause wonders in the heavens above and signs on the earth below—blood and fire and clouds of smoke. The sun will become dark, and the moon will turn blood red before that great and glorious day of the Lord arrives. But everyone who calls on the name of the Lord will be saved.'"

Acts 2:2

"Death is swallowed up in victory...Sin is the sting that results in death, and the law gives sin its power. But, thank God! He gives us victory over sin and death through our Lord Jesus Christ."

1 Corinthians 15:54–57

"In this way, He disarmed the spiritual rulers and authorities. He shamed them publicly by His victory over them on the cross."

Colossians 2:15

Ride a Cock Horse

Ride a cock horse to Bambury cross,
to see a fine lady upon a white horse;
with rings on her fingers and bells on her toes,
she shall have music wherever she goes.

Ride a Colt Horse

Ride a colt horse to Calvary's Cross!
They see their fine Saviour upon a meek horse;
they bring him palm fringes, and
lay out their clothes.
He shall have music wherever He goes.

Ride a colt horse to Calvary's cross!
But see the crowd change as it gathers in force.
It sings to begin with, then yells with His foes,
"Crucify Jesus!" The clamoring grows.

Ride a colt horse to Calvary's cross!
We see our great Saviour, full set on His course
to willingly bring us from hell's deathly blows.
Hark Heaven's music! In victory He rose!

"…They brought the colt to Jesus…As he rode along, the crowds spread out their garments along the road ahead of him…they…began to shout and sing…praising God."

Luke 19:28–40

"A large crowd…took palm branches and…shouted, 'Praise God!…Hail to the King of Israel!'…Jesus found a young donkey and rode on it, fulfilling the prophesy."

John 12:12–16

"Then a mighty roar rose from the crowd, and with one voice they shouted, 'Kill Him! and release Barabbus to us!'…They kept shouting, 'Crucify Him! Crucify Him!'…The mob shouted louder and louder, demanding that Jesus be crucified, and their voices prevailed."

Luke 23:18–25

"…I heard the voices of thousands and millions of angels…and they sang…'Worthy is the Lamb who was slaughtered…blessing and honour and glory and power belong to the one sitting on the throne.'"

Revelation 5:11–14

Pat-a-Cake

Pat-a-cake, pat-a-cake,
baker's man,
bake me a cake
as fast as you can.
Pat it and prick it
and mark it with "B,"
and put it in the oven
for Baby and me.

Bread of Life

Bread of Life, Bread of Life,
God made man;
taken, forsak'n,
outcast, so I can
take it, and eat it,
and make it for me,
and, partaking with others,
may they be set free!

"I am the Bread of Life! ... Anyone who eats the Bread from Heaven ... will never die ... and this bread, which I will offer so the world may live, is my flesh."

John 6:47–51

" ... He was despised and rejected ... He was pierced for our rebellion, crushed for our sins ... He was beaten so we could be whole. He was whipped so we could be healed ... He was oppressed and treated harshly ... unjustly condemned, he was led away ..."

Isaiah 53:3–12

"Jesus said, 'Take this and share it among yourselves ... This is my body, which is given for you. Do this to remember me.'"

Luke 22:7–20

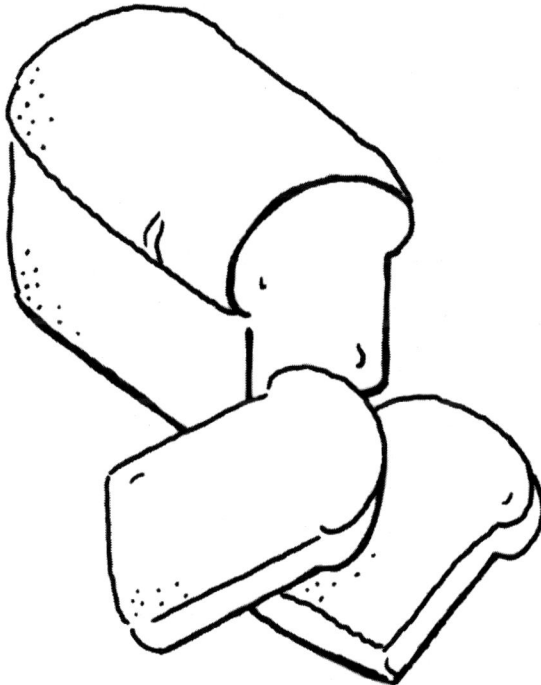

Round and Round the Garden

Round and round the garden
like a teddy bear.
One step, two steps!
Tickley under there.

Round and Round the Garden

Round and round the garden,
bitter tears and prayer.
One step, two steps,
suffering hard to bear!

Round and round the garden
Christ so longs to share.
One step, two steps,
don't they even care?

Resting in the garden,
friends sleep unawares.
One step, two steps,
He for death prepares.

"Jesus went ... to the olive grove ... he became anguished and distressed ... He went on a little farther, and bowed his face to the ground, praying.... Then He returned to the disciples and found them asleep ... He said ..., 'Couldn't you watch with me even one hour?'...Jesus left them a second time and prayed ... When He returned to them again, He found them sleeping ... He went to pray a third time ... Then he came to the disciples and said ... 'The Son of man is betrayed ...!'"

Matthew 26:36–45

Three Blind Mice

Three blind mice,
see how they run!
They all run after
the farmer's wife,
who cut off their tails
with a carving knife.
Did ever you see
such a thing in your life
as three blind mice?

Three Blind Guys

Three blind guys,
see how they run!
They all run after
a "charmer's" life;
temptation prevails,
causing harm and strife.
They never could see
what it did to their life;
these three blind guys.

Remind guys
where they should run.
Should all run after
the Source of light,
who takes off the scales
and restores their sight.
Did ever you see
such a thing of delight?
Let's remind guys!

"They began to think up foolish ideas ... as a result their minds became dark and confused."

Romans 1:21–24, 29–32

"Satan, who is the god of this world, has blinded the minds of those who don't believe. They are unable to see the glorious light of the Good News ... God who said, 'Let there be light in the darkness' has made this light shine in our hearts ..."

2 Corinthians 4:3–7

"Jesus ... said, 'I am the light of the world. If you follow me you won't have to walk in darkness, because you will have the light that leads to life.'"

John 8:12

The Queen of Hearts

The Queen of Hearts
she made some tarts
all on a summer's day.
The Knave of Hearts,
he stole those tarts,
and took them clean away.

The King of Hearts
called for those tarts,
and beat the knave full sore.
The Knave of Hearts
brought back the tarts,
and vowed he'd steal no more.

The King of Hearts

The king of Hearts
He gives new starts
to those who seek His way.
The knave of Hearts
would stop those starts
and lead the folk astray.

The Prince of Hearts
though killed, restarts
and beats the knave full sore.
The knave of Hearts,
thus beat, departs,
and wields his power no more.

" ...Anyone who belongs to Christ has become a new person. The old life has gone; a new life has begun!"

2 Corinthians 5:17

"For I am afraid that some of them have already gone astray, and now follow Satan."

1 Timothy 5:15

" ...[Christ] ...died ...to break the power of sin ..."

Romans 6:10

" ...He seized ...Satan, and bound him in chains ...threw him into the bottomless pit, which he then shut and locked so Satan could not deceive the nations anymore ..."

Revelations 20:2–3

Jack and Jill

Jack and Jill climbed up the hill
to fetch a pail of water.
Jack fell down and broke his crown,
and Jill came tumbling after.
Up Jack got and home did trot
as fast as he could caper.
He went to bed to mend his head
with vinegar and brown paper.

Jack and Jill

Jack and Jill climbed up the hill
of "doing what they oughta."
Both fell down and broke their crowns,
and we came tumbling after.
We could not, no matter what,
get past our first few capers.
Self has led our heart and head;
To sin again's in our natures.

Christ fulfilled God's total will,
but man cried for his slaughter!
Beaten down, with thorny crown,
they led him stumbling after.
Shared this plot, "Now let's be shot
of this man and His capers!
We've lost our cred through what He said,
this sinner man shan't escape us!"

When they killed Him on that hill
He bore the sin that thwarts us.
Then, Heav'n bound, with glory crowned,
sent death a-tumbling after!
Sin that stopped us being what
we first of all were made for
fell instead on Jesus' head—
So! Begin again—all is paid for!

"So it is clear that no one can be made right with God by trying to keep the law."

Galatians 3:11

"I know that nothing good lives in…my sinful nature. I want to do what is right, but I can't…I don't want to do what is wrong, but I do it anyway."

Romans 7:18–21

"This High Priest of ours understands our weaknesses, for He faced all of the same testings we do, yet He did not sin."

Hebrews 4:15

"…The mob roared even loader, 'Crucify Him!'"

Matthew 27:23

"They wove thorn branches into a crown and put it on His head…they spit on Him, and grabbed the stick and struck Him on the head with it…and led Him away to be crucified."

Matthew 27:29–31

"The teachers of religious law and the leading priests wanted to arrest Jesus immediately because they realized He was telling the story against them."

Luke 20:19

"…the leading priests and elders were…plotting how to capture Jesus secretly and kill Him."

Matthew 26:3–4

"He personally carried our sins in his body on the cross so that we can be dead to sin and live for what is right. By his wounds you are healed."

1 Peter 2:24

"…Thank God! He gives us victory over sin and death through our Lord Jesus Christ."

1 Corinthians 15:57

Dr. Foster Went to Gloucester

Dr. Foster went to Gloucester
in a shower of rain.
He stepped in a puddle
right up to his middle,
and never went there again.

If You'd Lost a Coin
that Cost Yer

If you'd lost a coin that cost yer
all your earthly gain,
you'd clear up your muddle,
and make sure you did all
to find that lost coin again.

God still searches, and His church is
full of "lost reclaimed."
"Come sing!" He will bid all,
"Play trumpet and fiddle!
A sinner is found again!"

"Suppose a woman has ten coins and she loses one. Won't she light a lamp and sweep the entire house and search carefully until she finds it? And when she finds it, she will call in her friends and neighbours and say, 'Rejoice with me because I have found my lost coin!' In the same way, there is joy in the presence of God's angels when even one sinner repents."

Luke 15:8–10

See-Saw, Margery Daw

See-saw, Margery Daw,
Johnny shall have a new master.
He shall have but a penny a day,
because he can't work any faster.

See-Saw, Margery Daw

See-saw, Margery Daw,
choosing who'll be her new master.
She may choose to serve pennies each day,
and then as she works they grow faster.

See saw, Margery Daw,
she may choose God as her Master.
She's aware that there's many a day,
His love helps her cope with disaster.

See saw, Margery Daw,
cannot serve both as her master.
One she'd hate, and the other obey;
and always do all that He asked her.

"No one can serve two masters. For you will hate one and love the other; you will be devoted to one and despise the other. You cannot serve both God and money."

Matthew 6:24

Ding Dong Bell

Ding dong bell,
Pussy's in the well.
"Who put her in?"
Little Johnny Green.
"Who pulled her out?"
Little Tommy Stout.
What a naughty boy was that
to try to drown poor pussy cat,
who never did him any harm,
and killed the mice in his father's barn.

Ding Dong Bell

Ding dong bell,
woman at the well.
"Where had she been?"
Living in great sin.
"Who sought her out?"
Jesus without doubt
knew her wicked life and that
she tried to drown her guilt with "chat,"
she tried so hard to play a part,
not thinking twice of His "Father heart."

Ding dong bell,
Jesus at the well.
"What did he say?"
"Let me drink, I pray!"
"What did he do?"
Said, "I offer you
drink that bubbles from inside,
a living stream that's never dried;
it heals your hurt like gentle balm
and fills your life with my lasting calm."

" … Jesus sat beside the well … soon a Samaritan woman came to draw water … Jesus said … 'Please give me a drink … If you only knew the gift God has for you and who you are speaking to, you would ask me, and I would give you living water … Those who drink the water I give them will never be thirsty again. It becomes a fresh, bubbling spring within them, giving them eternal life.'"

"Jesus said, 'You're right! … You have had five husbands, and you aren't even married to the man you are living with now …'"

" … The woman said, ' … Why is it that you Jews insist that Jerusalem is the only place of worship, while we Samaritans claim it is here … where our ancestors worshiped?' Jesus replied, ' … It will no longer matter' … The woman said, 'I know the Messiah is coming … He will explain everything to us.' Then Jesus told her, 'I am the Messiah!'"

John 4:4–26

Tom, Tom, the Piper's Son

Tom, Tom, the piper's son
stole a pig and away did run.
The pig was eat
and Tom was beat,
and he went crying down the street.

Paul, Paul, A Jewish Son

Paul, Paul, a Jewish son
Told the world that Christ had come.
This stirred up heat
And Paul was beat,
'Cos he preached Jesus in the street.

" …We decided to leave for Macedonia at once, having concluded that God was calling us to preach the Good News there."

Acts 16:10

" …They grabbed Paul…and dragged them before the authorities …'The whole city is in an uproar because of these Jews!' they shouted to the city officials …A mob quickly formed against Paul and Silas and the city officials ordered them stripped and beaten with rods. They were severely beaten, and then they were thrown into prison…The jailer put them into the inner dungeon and clamped their feet in stocks."

Acts 16:16–24

Goosey, Goosey Gander

Goosey, goosey gander
whither will you wander?
Upstairs, downstairs,
in my lady's chamber.
There I met an old man
who wouldn't say his prayers.
I took him by the left leg
and threw him down the stairs.

Useless, You Meander

Useless, you meander,
willingly you wander
this way, that way,
to all opinions pander.
If you meet an old man
and false ideas he shares,
you shift from right to left leg.
For truth? Who really cares?

F' sooth, the truth I'll ponder,
wishing not to flounder.
God shares my cares
in my inner chamber.
There I meet with "God—Man"
who listens to my prayers.
"I AM the life, the one way,
One truth," he then declares.

"Do not waver, for a person with divided loyalty is as unsettled as a wave of the sea that is blown and tossed by the wind...they are unstable in everything they do."

James 1:6

"How much longer will you waver, hobbling between two opinions? If the Lord is God, follow Him! But if Baal is God then follow him!"

1 Kings 18:21

"Choose today whom you will serve...but as for me and my family, we will serve the Lord."

Joshua 24:15

"When you pray, go away by yourself, shut the door behind you, and pray to your Father in private...Your Father knows exactly what you need."

Matthew 6:6–7

"Jesus said, 'I am the way, the truth and the life. No one can come to the Father except through me.'"

John 14:6

Hickory Dickory Dock

Hickory Dickory Dock!
The mouse ran up the clock.
The clock struck one,
the mouse ran down.
Hickory Dickory Dock!

Hickory Dickory Dock

Hickory Dickory Dock!
Your life runs like a clock.
When time is done,
and race is run,
will you be quickest, or not?

Hickory Dickory Dock!
The storm comes as a shock!
When rains beats down,
and you could drown,
built on the silt or the rock?

Hickory Dickory Dock!
The shepherd sorts his flock.
"Sheep! In you come!
You goats go down!"
Which of the pick is your lot?

This is a visitor's knock
You daren't ignore or mock.
Christ stands before
your heart's closed door.
Click the key quick and unlock.

"Don't you realize that in a race everyone runs but only one person gets the prize? So run to win!"

1 Corinthians 9:24

"Anyone who listens to my teaching and follows it is wise, like a person who builds a house on solid rock...Though the rain comes...and the floodwaters rise...it won't collapse...Anyone who hears my teaching and ignores it is foolish, like a person who builds a house on sand...when the rains and floods come...it will collapse."

Matthew 7:24–27

"He will separate the people as a shepherd separates the sheep from the goats.... Sheep at his right hand...goats at his left...The King will say to those on the right, 'Come...inherit the Kingdom...' Then to those on the left...'Away with you...'"

Matthew 25:32–46

"I stand at the door and knock. If you hear my voice and open the door, I will come in, and we will share a meal together as friends."

Revelation 3:20

Diddle Diddle Dumpling

Diddle, diddle dumpling;
my son John
Went to bed with his trousers on!
One shoe off and one shoe on.
Diddle, diddle dumpling, my son John.

Tittle Tattle, Grumbling

Tittle tattle, grumbling, lies are spun;
rumours spread, and the row's begun;
peace is off and war is on!
Did all this all come from my small tongue?

"The tongue is a small thing that makes grand speeches...but a tiny spark can set a great forest on fire. And the tongue is a flame of fire. It is a whole world of wickedness, corrupting your whole body. It can set your whole life on fire...People can tame all kinds of animals...but no one can tame the tongue."

James 3:2–12

Hey Diddle Diddle

Hey diddle, diddle,
the cat and the fiddle,
the cow jumped over the moon!
The little dog laughed
to see such sport
and the dish ran away with the spoon!

Hey Diddle Diddle

Hey diddle, diddle,
explain this great riddle,
the lame are over the moon!
The blind and deaf laugh,
for Jesus taught
it's God's wish the oppressed
are freed soon.

"Jesus told them, 'Go back to John and tell him what you have heard and seen—the blind see, the lame walk, the lepers are cured, the deaf hear, the dead are raised to life, and the Good News is being preached to the poor.'"

Matthew 11:4–5

"'…He has sent me to proclaim that captives will be released, that the blind will see, and the oppressed will be set free, and that the time of the Lord's favour has come…The scriptures that you have just heard have been fulfilled this very day!'"

Luke 4:17–21

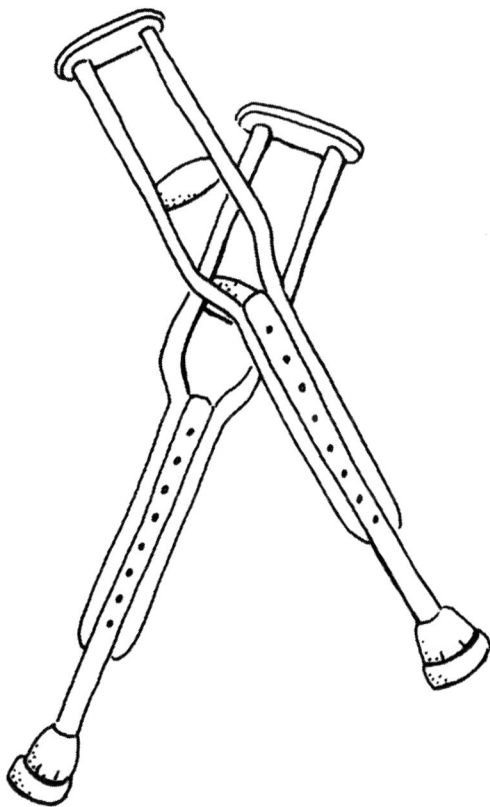

Jack Sprat

Jack Sprat could eat no fat;
his wife could eat no lean;
and so between them both, you see,
they licked the platter clean.

Fleet Feet

Fleet feet can eat no meat,
and eyes can never talk.
The nose between them cannot see,
and ears just cannot walk.

Ears hear and eyes can peer;
we need the nose to smell;
and so between them all, you see,
the body functions well.

"The human body has many parts, but the many parts make up one whole body...if the whole body were an eye, how would you hear? Or if your whole body were an ear, how would you smell anything?...God has put each part just where He wants it...The eye can never say to the hand, "I don't need you"...The head can't say to the feet, 'I don't need you!.'...This makes for harmony among the members, so that all the members care for each other."

1 Corinthians 12:12–27

Pease Porridge Hot

Pease porridge hot,
pease porridge cold,
pease porridge in the pot
nine days old.
Some like it hot,
some like it cold,
some like it in the pot,
nine days old.

Some Churches Hot

Some churches hot,
some churches cold,
some Christians' love has got
tired and old.
When it's not hot
nor is it cold,
God rejects what they've got,
but gives gold.

"Write this letter to ... the church ... I know ... that you are neither hot nor cold ... since you are lukewarm ... neither hot nor cold, I will spit you out of my mouth! ... I advise you to buy gold from me—gold that has been purified by fire. Then you will be rich."

Revelation 3:14–22

Old King Cole

Old King Cole
was a merry old soul,
and a merry old soul was he!
He called for his pipe
and he called for his bowl
and he called for his fiddlers three.

Old King Cole

Old King Cole
was a merry old soul,
and yet merrier souls are we!
God calls—not His "type,"
but He calls to us all!
At His ball He has bid us all be!

"A king…prepared a great wedding feast…'…The guests I invited aren't worthy of the honour. Now go out to the street corners and invite everyone you see.' So the servants brought in everyone they could find, good and bad alike and the banquet hall was filled with guests."

Matthew 22:1–10

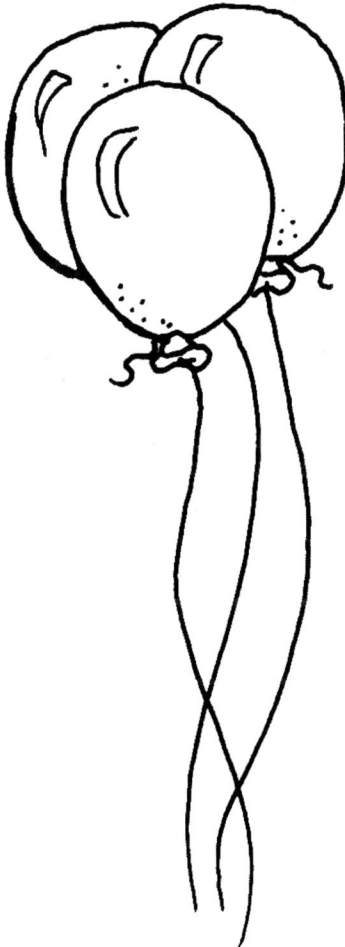

Wee Willie Winkie

Wee Willie Winkie
runs through the town,
upstairs and downstairs
in his nightgown,
rapping at the window,
crying through the lock,
"Are the children all in bed,
for now it's eight o'clock?"

We Will Be Thinking

We will be thinking,
when doubts abound,
"Who shares in our cares
when we're right down?"
Grappling with their sin, those
crying should take stock;
for the children God has led
are safe upon His rock!

"O Lord, how long will you forget me? Forever? How long will you look the other way? How long must I struggle with anguish in my soul, with sorrow in my heart every day? ...But I trust in your unfailing love. I will rejoice because you have rescued me. I will sing to the Lord because He is good to me."

Psalm 13

"O God, listen to my cry! Hear my prayer! From the ends of the earth I cry to you for help when my heart is overwhelmed. Lead me to the towering rock of safety, for you are my safe refuge, a fortress where my enemies can't reach me."

Psalm 61